# BROETRY

# Broetry

## Poetry for Dudes

BRIAN MCGACKIN

QUIRK BOOKS
PHILADELPHIA

Library of Congress Cataloging in Publication Number: 2011922700

ISBN: 978-1-59474-517-1

Printed in China

Typeset in Bembo

Designed by Doogie Horner
Illustrations by Lars Leetaru
Production management by John J. McGurk

Quirk Books
215 Church Street
Philadelphia, PA 19106
quirkbooks.com

10 9 8 7 6 5 4 3 2 1

THIS BOOK IS DEDICATED TO

MARGARET AGNES CONNELLY,

THE MOST BEAUTIFUL

WOMAN IN THE WORLD.

Introduction                                          11

## High School to Hangovers

## Sophomoronic

## Girls, Girls, Graduation

## Extreme Poverty Is the New Poverty

## Twenty-Five to Life

# Introduction

Broetry originated centuries ago, high atop the mountains of feudal Japan, when a small sect of samurai monks decided they were tired of writing poems that were deep and meaningful, and opted instead to write something people might actually enjoy.

Okay, I made all of that up. Broetry is poetry for dudes. It's poetry for people who don't like poetry. Had a rough day? Feel like sitting down and relaxing but only have a few minutes before the girlfriend gets back from Pilates? Broetry.

It's a versatile form. Regular poetry is all about birds and death, birch trees and fancy words. The broetic world, on the other hand, encompasses manlier topics, like beer, sex, video games, sports, celebrities, and songs you can't get out of your head even though you're not quite sure how they got there in the first place. Broetry is poetry for the twenty-first century. Broetry speaks to every man, woman, and dude-child who understands that reading shouldn't have to be a chore.

A poet I admire once wrote, "Saying you don't like poetry is like saying you don't like food." In other words, a beet is just a beet. If you're not into beets, you can eat spinach. Don't like vegetables? Have pizza! The point is, if you think you don't like poetry, you just haven't found a poem that's right for you.

Broetry is poetry that's right for you.

Broetry is a literary chili cheeseburger.

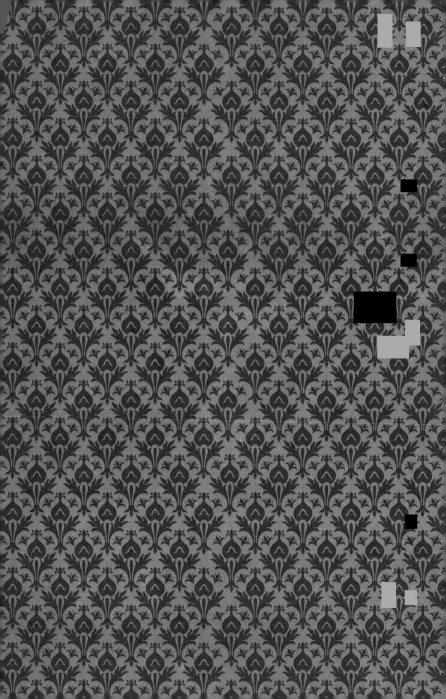

# HIGH SCHOOL

## TO

# HANGOVERS

# Lying in a Sleeping Bag in Nicole Sanchez's Basement, Prom Night 2003

Over my head, I see worn ski equipment,
two cracked snowboards, and a black kayak
strung from wooden beams across the ceiling.
Down near my feet, I hear the snores
of other couples, passed out early
after too many Smirnoff Ices.
To my right,
in a field of moonlight cast through the only window,
a girl I didn't know last year breathes
softly against my bare shoulder.
I lean back, as the sounds of others making out die away.
A small hand floats across my chest,
a girl smiles in her sleep.
Never date a freshman.

# Move In

We're not even out of the car yet, but
I've already been secretly searching.
Pull up, park, campus greeter (no). Unpack,
too much crap, elevator (almost, no).

Extra-long twin sheets, toothpaste, microwave,
make sure to get the whiteboard up, make space
for the roommate's stuff, RA (no again),

mini-fridge. Lunch break, dining hall. First time:
nothing good. It has to get better, right?
So many other things should be on my
mind—books, classes, friends—and I honestly

don't know when I might see my mom again,
but all at once the next four years look fine:
well, that girl across the hall does at least.

# Not Another Teen Movie

Never
Been
Kissed.

Waiting. . . .
Les Misérables.
The Opposite of Sex.

Thirteen. Chain Reaction.
One Fine Day. The Arrival. Savior.
The Girl Next Door. She's All That.
Lovely & Amazing. The Object of My Affection.
Mission: Impossible. Fools Rush In. Whatever It Takes.

Contact. Nothing to Lose.
The Game. Catch Me If You Can.
50 First Dates. The Rules of Attraction. Be Cool.
28 Days Later.
Closer. Meet the Parents. Bring It On.

Head Over Heels.
A Lot Like Love.
America's Sweethearts.
As Good as It Gets.
Pleasantville.
Life Is Beautiful.

Romeo + Juliet.

Picture Perfect.
Love Actually.
Ever After.
The One.

Let's Talk about Sex.
Can't Hardly Wait.
Great Expectations.
In the Bedroom.
That Thing You Do.
Private Parts. Snatch. Shaft.
Deep Impact. Supernova. O. Goal!
I Am Legend.
PS I Love You.

40 Days and 40 Nights.
Varsity Blues. The Edge. Accepted.
The Last Days. Addicted to Love.
Goodbye Lover.
Gone Baby Gone. Return to Me.

Dead Man on Campus.
Meeting People Is Easy.
The Missing. Out of Sight.
The Next Best Thing. Human Nature.
Flirting with Disaster.
Dangerous Ground. Dangerous Beauty.
Drop Dead Gorgeous. Simply Irresistible.
All Over Me. Fire Down Below.
Striptease. One Night Stand.

Abandon. Disturbing Behavior.
Wild Things. Very Bad Things. Unfaithful.

I Know What You Did Last Summer.
Dick. Monster. Scream. Panic.
Liar Liar. Big Fat Liar.
Thirteen Conversations about One Thing.
War. Armageddon. The Break-Up. Go.
Independence Day.
The Grudge. Cruel Intentions. Romeo Must Die.
10 Things I Hate About You.
Y Tu Mamá También.
Intolerable Cruelty. Psycho. Desperate Measures.
Two Can Play That Game.
The New Guy. Next. The Others. Rebound.
Crash. Boys Don't Cry. Down with Love. Stuck on You.
Insomnia.

28 Weeks Later.
The Bachelor. The Ex.
Blast from the Past. Serendipity. Still Crazy.
Enough. Get Over It.
The Peacemaker. How to Deal. Adaptation. Atonement.
A Walk to Remember. Joy Ride.
Booty Call. Frequency. Honey. Beloved.
Bad Company. Exit Wounds.
I Still Know What You Did Last Summer.
I'll Always Know What You Did Last Summer.
The End of the Affair.
The Last Kiss. Memento.

Final Destination.
Just Friends. Serenity.
Why Do Fools Fall in Love?

# I'll Take "Crazy Bitches" for $200, Alex

*Beating out several prominent
one-night stands, she was named
"Craziest Bitch of the Year"
in 2005 and 2007.*

Who is my ex-girlfriend?

*Right.*

"Crazy Bitches" for $400.

*Usually referred to as "zero,"
"nonexistent," or "the same as that of
Hell freezing over," her family still
calls it "pretty good."*

What are the odds of us
getting back together?

*Correct.*

"Bitches" for $600.

*The sex was great.*

What is the only reason we stayed
together for so long?

*Yes.*

"Crazy Bitches" for $800, Alex.

*Answer: Daily Double!*
*You've got an opportunity to take*
*the lead.*

I'll wager $2400.

*That'll put you ahead of all your*
*opponents. Here is your clue:*
*Youreanasshole.*

What is . . . the capital of Idontgiveafuck?

*That's the one, putting*
*you in the lead by $800.*

Let's go with "Crazy Bitches" for $1000.

*I hate you,*
*but I can't hate you,*
*because I love you.*

What is wrong with you?

*You got it.*

I'll take "Times I Got So Drunk I Puked
on a National Monument" for $200, please.

# Now I Assume That Everyone Named Harry Is a Wizard

Cold, late night so long ago,
some girl said, "These are good, you know."
She handed me a novel;
it looked really fucking dumb.
I put it off for several weeks—
back then I wasn't such a geek.
Actually, that's bullshit. I was worse and I know it.

"Come on, read it," she flirted and cooed.
"You don't have to love it, though it is really good."
So try to understand . . .
Try to understand . . .
Try, try, try to understand . . .
I was fifteen and she was really cute.

Days and days I read and read,
just to get this girl in bed.
"Wingardium leviosa. Alohomora."
So, once I'd finished every one
I went to tell her what I'd done.
Ya know, I had to admit that I really enjoyed it.

"Then come along, please," she begged with a pout.
"I need someone to join me when the new book
        comes out.
But try to understand . . .

Try to understand . . .
Try, try, try to understand . . .
It means dressing like wizards in public."

*~pensive moment/actually considering it/musical interlude~*

"Come on! No way!" I said to that chick.
"Yeah, I'd like to fuck you, sure, but this is ridic.
But try to understand . . .
Try to understand . . .
Try, try, try to understand . . .
You can totally call me when you're done."

*~another thoughtful moment of silence/longer interlude this
time~*

"Please come with me," she finally said.
"Maybe, if you're good, we'll go and read in my bed."
So try to understand . . .
Try to understand . . .
Try, try, try to understand . . .

# Close

Hot girls who smoke are
like luxury vehicles
with busted fenders.

# But No

Hot girls who smoke are
like milk that's a day too old,
but taste even worse.

# Cigar

Hot girls who smoke are
still hot, don't get me wrong, but
I wouldn't fuck one.

# Whorecrux

I have halved my heart seven times, but now
all I can find of the pieces are these
quasi-emo memories:

    In first grade
this cute redhead and I would share Snack Packs.
She dumped me one recess, and now I can't
bring myself to ever date a ginger.
Their hair reminds me of how my heart was
tossed aside like a red tin-foil lid;
their pale skin is a shameful reminder
of that ill-boding vanilla pudding.

I also will not eat tapioca,
but that's for a much different reason.

Although I LOVE rice pudding. Anyway—

The next siren to rip apart my soul
came along in middle school. Our first kiss
was accompanied by raucous applause
during a scandalous Valentine's Day
game of Spin the Bottle; we hit it off
instantly a month later. We went on
awkward dates to movies like *Titanic,*
*The Wedding Singer, Liar Liar,* and
*The Fifth Element.* It was all too cute
for words, clearly. But then, just like before,

she broke up with me seemingly out of
nowhere. She said I talked too much about
Bruce Willis's awesomeness during the
movie, and it annoyed her. To this day
I still can't look at Milla Jovovich
without thinking of whatever her name
was. And duct tape.

Girl number three made me
read *Harry Potter* with her, which was fine—
until the first movie came out. What I
was prepared to write off as a minor
difference of opinion she thought was
more of a major, insurmountable
character flaw. Whatever, she was prude.

Girl Four broke up with me on my birthday.
I have no idea why.

Girl Five was great,
but she somehow met Girl Four, even though
they lived in different towns and went to
different schools—and honestly folks, this
was back in AOL days, so who knows
how these bitches found each other—and then
they decided together that Girl Five
had the same mystery problem that Girl
Four had, so there that went.

        Despite what she
promised when she signed my yearbook, Five did
not "keep in touch." The last I heard, the two
of them were still really close and thinking
about moving out to San Francisco.

This may sound stupid, but I dumped Girl Six.
She didn't want to hang out with me much
after that, which was a bummer because
she was really cool. Except for the late
night phone calls. And jealous text messages.
The random fits of rage sucked, too, I guess.
And she could be kind of a hypocrite
sometimes, which wasn't fun. And she hated
all of my female friends, so that took some
getting used to at first, especially
since she only had guy friends. Oh, and she
had this strange tendency to cheat on me.
No big. We were in love, what can I say?

Oh, Seven. Seven, Seven, Seven. Sigh.
Seven was more of a dog than a girl.
No, like an actual dog, a canine.
Delilah, my longest relationship by far,
(even longer, counting dog years). That bitch
was crazy for me. She was the only
girl ever allowed in my room, and she
didn't mind walking around naked all
the time, unlike One, Two, Four, Five, and Six.
She never nagged me, or asked where I was

going at night, or refused to cuddle
if I stayed out too late and didn't call.
She'd let me play video games all day
as long as I let her lie her head down
on my lap. She even loved comic books,
though more the taste than the content.

    If she
had one flaw, it was loving me too much.
One weekend I came home from college and
she was so excited to see me that
she ran out into the road to greet me
at the car.

    We buried her body in
the backyard beneath her favorite tree.
It's a very nice tree.

# Stopping by Wawa
# on a Snowy Evening

Is Wawa open? Yes or no?
We need to stop if it's not closed
To stock up for the party. Shit!
But Wawa doesn't sell beer, though.

I'm such an ass. I must admit
I'd completely forgotten it:
Convenience stores don't sell booze here.
Now how the hell will we get lit?

We've only got two racks of beer
And one bottle of Everclear;
That's just enough for maybe three
Or four of us. It would appear

That some of us will have to be
Spending the night alcohol-free.
I guess I'll drink lemonade tea,
I guess I'll drink lemonade tea.

# My Mom's Basement

It doesn't have carpeting or parquet
floors. There's no HDTV set up so
me and my friends can watch blu-ray
on my PS3. I would love for there to be
some type of Bowflex, or family gaming
table even, so I could drop some serious
Scrabble knowledge on all y'all's asses,
but it's just not gonna happen. Sorry.

Not even a mini-fridge filled with Dew
to down while I pwn n00bs on WoW for hours,
or go old school and rock out with my
RC-P90 out in *Goldeneye* (I call Oddjob).
It's actually filled with tons of useless crap,
like a normal basement. Broken Ninja Turtles,
a bassinet, laundry, some musty Halloween robes.
I made a pretty sweet fort down there once, though.

# THURSDAY, Part 1

## Anticipation

I'm not an alcoholic—
at least, I'm pretty sure; though,
my mother tends to leave the porch
light on more and more these days—

well, when I'm there, anyway—
but some bar nights, or parties,
maybe Labor Day BBQs,
parade themselves through my mind

weeks ahead of time, like prom,
or the first day of college.
I get Disney World excited
for the weekend's first Guinness

sometimes, when it's been a while,
or if I've had a rough hour.

# THURSDAY, Part 2

## The Buzz

It goes down rough, but oh Christ,
that's good. I never thought that
standing could feel so much like a
massage. One more shot real quick.

Huh? Oh hey! My man! What's up?
How's it been, man, good? Yeah? Good.
No, no, same shit, just hanging out,
you know how it is—hold up—

what? Who is this? Wait, I can't—
oh, yeah yeah, I'll buzz you in.
See ya. Hey sorry. Here, drink this.
Wow, that is fantastic. This

is great, I had no idea
so many people would show.

# THURSDAY, Part 3

## Drunk

Who the fuck are these people?
Beer! Man, you guys read my minds.
Who are you, like, the Beer Fairy?
That's so great, thanks for coming.

Seriously, who are you?
No way! Yeah yeah yeah, okay.
I fucking love that rat bastard
Here, throw me one of them beers.

Oh shit, my bad. Just use that
towel there. Whose turn is it?
Wait, when the fuck did that happen?
So play again. Play again!

Hold up, whose water is this?
Hell no, $H_2O$! Let's play.

# THURSDAY, Part 4

## The Sleep

Eight plus four plus I think three
equals—I can't count that high—
How many cups of water that?
Is that? How much cups—just pour.

Can we go to bed now? No,
I wasn't—I was talking
to God. The ceiling is being
mean when I close my eyes so

I'm just gonna tell God on him.
What are you—that's not a wall!
No, it's not, it's—oh shit! Haha!
I thought the desk was tired!

Yeah, no, wait, bed is not fun.
I am so fucked up right now.

# THURSDAY, Part 5

**Morning**

Never. Again.

# SOPHOMORONIC

# Tidal Wave Dream

You ever have one of those fucked up dreams
where you're playing poker with Bruce Willis
and that one hot chick from *Step by Step*
when all of a sudden a tidal wave comes
crashing through Big Bird's house forcing you
to surf him to the top of the Prudential Center
in Boston and just chill there with three homeless
gymnasts and a bald eagle until the water recedes
even though you were in Seattle when
the tidal wave hit and you know this because
you had an entire conversation with Bruce Willis
about how you'd never been to Seattle before
and why *Twilight* is the dumbest book ever?
No reason. A simple *yes* or *no* would suffice.

# The Guttenberg Bible

In the beginning God created heaven and
Steve Guttenberg, and God saw that it was good,

so He let Steve take care of the rest. And Steve said,
"Let there be light," and there was light. And Steve said,

"Let there be *Police Academies*," and there were
six sequels. And then, in a moment of true

genius, Steve said, "Let there be Tom Selleck and Ted
Danson," and there were *Three Men and a Baby*.

And Steve saw that it was good. It was so, so good.
And God was pleased, and all was right with the world.

But then Steve said, "Let there be *High Spirits*," and,
"Let there be *It Takes Two*," and finally, for some

strange reason, "Let there be *Zeus and Roxanne*, about
a dog and a dolphin who become best friends,

wouldn't that be so cool? Guys? God? Anybody?"
And it was not good. It was not good at all.

(I know because I saw it in theaters when
I was eleven; even then I knew it sucked.)

So then Steve said, "Let there be *Dancing with the Stars*,"
but by that point God had stopped listening long,

long ago, and Steve was on his own. Maybe he
should have considered a job in publishing;

I hear Gutenberg is a good name for that.

# Ode to That Girl I Dated for, Like, a Month Sophomore Year

I used to think about you, or one-night
stands I've had, and wonder if you were my
best chance at happiness someday, in an
alternate future, similar to when
I'd wonder if my best possible child

died inside my ex-girlfriend's mouth. It's an
idle, vagrant thought, stuck now in the
gray marble government building of my brain,
at unemployment, in line behind my
memories of little league and my dreams

of becoming an astronaut. I ask:
*How have you been on your own? Have you looked
for work, one-month-memory girl? Have you
gone to great lengths to keep yourself employed?
relevant? Young and smooth and enticing?*

You're lost there, between forgotten-name girl
and one-night-stand girl, jostling for more than
your perpetual position in line,
stranded in a waiting room out of time.

# Golden Grahams

Crammed with graham, and other cool stuff. Stuff like:
whole grain wheat; sugar; corn meal; brown sugar syrup;
canola and/or rice bran oil; dextrose; baking soda; salt;
trisodium phosphate; artificial flavor; BHT added to pre-
serve freshness; freshness; 25% of the average Daily Value of
folic acid; trace amounts of crack cocaine; something that
makes me swear my mouth is having sex with a graham
cracker beehive; calcium carbonate; fond memories of my
ex-girlfriend's parents, who used to make sure there was
always a box in their pantry to satisfy a growing teenage
boy like myself in ways that their daughter wasn't already
doing so; adequately fond memories of my ex-girlfriend as
well, I suppose; a sense of achievement at being able to call
myself an adult, support myself financially, and choose
whatever cereal I damn well please because I'm a man and
I said so; delusions that anyone gives a shit what cereal I
buy; Zinc and Iron; those little ridges that keep the grahams from getting soggy too soon; shamefully high levels
of sodium; an evolutionary trigger that manifests itself as a
predisposition toward developing positive taste responses
to Cinnamon Toast Crunch and, to a lesser extent, French
Toast Crunch, if the subject's parents are willing to pur-
chase the former and if the latter is still sold in stores; Thi-
amin, whatever the fuck that is; Riboflavin, which I'm
pretty sure is $B_2$; zero cholesterol; and, most importantly,
crunchy honey goodness.

# Kids Today

I hear FIFA in the other room,
but I've got too much work to do.
It's calling like a shot of whiskey
must have called dads back in the fifties.

My Grandpa had no video games,
*Kids today are spoiled!* he claims.
*When I was your age, I had two jobs!*
And what does he think I do, rob

liquor stores and laundromats?
Mug old ladies with a baseball bat?
Are laundromats even still around?
I do wash at my apartment now,

and I might not be an adult per se,
but I'm sure I'll make it there someday.

Theoretically.

# O Captain! My Captain America!

O Captain! my Captain! our fearful trip is done;
The Allied boys have reached Berlin, we've beaten back
    the Huns;
Now Hitler's out, that Sour Kraut, he shot himself or
    something,
And pretty soon we'll drop the bomb, those Japs could use
    a thumping:
    But O heart! heart! heart!
        O my friend, how can it be?
           So near the end my Captain's died,
              Fallen in the sea.


O Captain! my Captain! rise up and shake it off;
Rise up—and thaw your costume some—you've been
    gone long enough;
They found you in a block of ice—some poor old frozen
    stranger;
But now they'll have you lead their club, they'll call you
    an Avenger;
    Here Captain! dear partner!
        Oh wait, shit, never mind;
           There's been some kind of Civil War,
              You're dead again I find.


My Captain does not answer, his lips are pale and still;
They shot him on the courthouse steps, he has no pulse
    nor will;
At least this is a nobler death than drowning all alone;

The grave can wait, he'll lie in state, surrounded by his
   own;
      Exult, O shores, and ring, O bells!
      My Captain's heaven-sent,
         He shall finally find his—fuck!
            I think he's back again . . .

# No More Sticky Fingers

Self-adhesive girl can:
close herself at both ends;
stamp all strangers close friends;
cling to any slick man;
touch herself with both hands
up against a wall, then

throw herself away when
peeled off like white glue strands;
fasten any cracked span.
Who can say a heart bends
(never breaks) as it rends?
Self-adhesive girl can.

# Final Final Fantasy

I will not spend one hundred and thirteen
hours of my life on a video game
ever again. I will not rationalize,
claiming that it is somehow "research" for
my future career as a comic book
writer. I will not allow myself to be
sucked beyond the event horizon of an
RPG situated on a distant
planet, no matter how good the graphics are
on the nubile female lead character's chest.
I will no longer waste my time seeking out
arbitrary unlockable achievements.
I am going to start beating games faster.

# When Patrick Stewart Rules the World

I went to Future Rome and found
that rebels resurrected Caesar.
Antony they left in ground;
Cleopatra in a freezer.

I toured the city at my leisure—
almost everyone had fled—
Caesar couldn't blame them, either,
yet stayed to fight on in their stead.

He rose against the man who led
the Federation so despised.
The walls of New Vatican bled;
too many pilots met demise;

but none could long deter the rise
of he who helmed the *Enterprise*.

# The Road Unable to Be Taken Because I'm Trapped Behind a Line of Dudes in Stormtrooper Armor Who Feel the Need to Take Pictures with Every Girl They See Wearing a Slave Leia Outfit

Two panels both now in distant rooms,
as well as a rare signing with Stan,
but I cannot wade through these costumes.
This would be no issue, one assumes,
if only I were Multiple Man;

Then I could be most everywhere,
assimilate when my tasks are done,
continue on my way without a care;
though I'd learned all a mind could bear
my adventures would have just begun,

And one of my me's could simply lay
about and read, one watch TV.
Oh, I would finish more every day
than others could even think to say!
I doubt anyone should know more than me.

I shall be telling this with a sigh
somewhere hours and hours hence:
two panels, and multiples of I—
stuck here next to this smelly guy—
they would have made all the difference.

# Pocahotness

How wrong is it to be in love
with a cartoon character? I'm not
talking about spending hours
wasting away online, looking up toon
and hentai sites, anime wood
from fucked-up Japanese tentacle porn.
I'm talking about love, true love;
the kind of love that makes you want to be
an outdoorsman; the kind of love
that keeps you up at night thinking about
ways to animate yourself; love
that transcends race, language, time period,
basic physics, pixilation;
love that—Damn. Ariel's pretty hot, too . . .

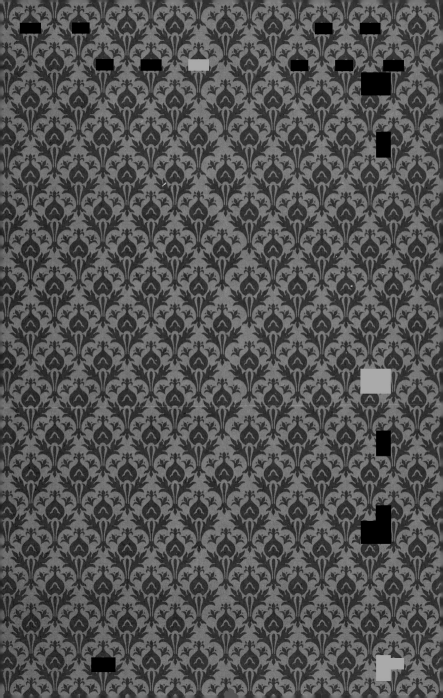

# GIRLS,
# GIRLS,
# GRADUATION

# Ode to Nicole Scherzinger; or, What's New, Pussycat?

I bet you've heard that one before.
Damn, when I saw you here I swore
I'd play it cool, maybe act tough,
you'd see me less like Derek Hough
and more the sort of scruffy guy

who drives your own pussy-cat wild.
I've got a kind of Eden's Crush—
no, wait a minute, that's too much.
I've got to try and hopefully
maintain some sense of dignity.

Unless that turns you on? Tell me,
what do you think? No? Possibly?
Maybe you like the nerdy type,
all nervous 'cus your clothes fit tight
around your ass and show your abs

without a single inch of flab;
and yet, your sexy silhouette,
the solid line beneath that dress,
your thighs, the way you shake your hips
like liquid sandstone, making this

cute guy tape *Dancing with the Stars*
so someday, when they grow up, our
children can see their mother's face,
they'll see your smile, aplomb, your grace,
the moment when you win first place.

I know that you don't need a man
but I'm no ordinary fan;
I'll stick with you until you see
our love is real, I'm not some creep.

# Morning Sex

The Belgian waffle of the sexual world.
Or maybe the McDonald's hash brown,
if that's more your type of breakfast item.
Both metaphors work for me. Don't judge.

Like breakfast in bed on your birthday, minus
the breakfast and/or restriction to special
occasions. It's pretty great when it happens
on your birthday, though, if you then get
breakfast in bed, too. That means you found a keeper.

Often utilized in affairs, new relationships, and
international business deals, since it successfully
       translates as,
"We can be late for work/class/your mother's brunch,"
in over forty-five languages, including ASL.
Especially ASL.

The easiest way to make your dreams come true,
particularly when one or both partners engage
before all parties involved have woken up.

Not a good idea if you've never before had sex
with the person you're sleeping next to, as it may
result in unexpected flatulence, disturbingly strong
morning breath, or legal action.

Alleged to be the scientifically optimal time
for a woman to experience pleasure from a man.
This theory still requires extensive research, though,
as I've only ever heard this claim from male scientists.

The single best way a man can start his day.
I'm not sure where it falls on the list for women.

# Haikougar

Cougar seduction
is not to be attempted
by the weekend flirt.

     A strong commitment
     is necessary to bag
     a fine specimen.

Wingmen, normally
helpful, are discouraged, since
they scare away prey.

     The first step is to
     determine the hunting grounds
     in your area.

Once you've discovered
your cougar den, be patient:
Wait for the right one.

     And by the "right one"
     I mean the hottest bitch you
     can possibly find.

Age, intelligence,
nationality—none of
that dumb shit matters.

     Ann Coulter is a
     right-wing conservative nut,
     but I'd still do her.

You must put away
these trivial thoughts if you
want to cougar hunt.

If you HAVE to know
her age, ask her where she was
when Kennedy died.
Hopefully she says,
"I was just a baby then,"
or "Wasn't born yet."
Teri Hatcher is
the perfect cougar: still hot,
born in '64.
She's just old enough
to be labeled a cougar,
but still looks damn good.
The older they are
the hotter they have to be
(or don't tell your friends).
A cougar over
sixty is fine, as long as
she's Helen Mirren.
Otherwise, don't waste
your time, 'cus seriously,
that's fucking gross, man.

# Jenga Fries

Generally an issue with crinkle
cut, but                    also found
to be problematic with string, waffle,
or any fry covered
in cheese (nacho or other), sour cream,
bacon, chili, or gravy.
Novice eaters lack the experience
necessary                  to navigate
potato terrain without assistance
     from a guide.
They choose inexpertly, often picking
fries frightfully distanced
from the top, just to avoid the ketchup.
     It is not wrong to correct them,
these daring disturbers at your table,
or even                    go so far as
to chastise them for defiling your fries.
Unless of course
the culprit is your girlfriend,
in which case you
should exercise
extreme
caution.

# Ode to Taylor Swift

I can't help it if you've looked like an angel
ever since you turned 18 (and just before,
too, God help me). You're only four years younger
than me, but at 2 a.m. when I'm online,
your website makes me feel like a creep.

But I'm okay with that, I think. The problem
comes when I'm at a bar and get too drunk and
sing along to "Love Story" or that "Our Song"
song, and all my friends yell, "Dude! You're gay!"
'cus singing teen-girl country is wrong.

But I'm okay with that, too, I guess. The real
issue to be addressed is when I'm sober
with no excuse. Today at the grocery
store I almost bought that *CosmoGirl* but caught
myself (I do have your *Women's Health*).

Marry me, Juliet. You'll never have to
hate my truck, I can't drive stick (I know, fucked up).
And I don't even like country, but you're still
the reason for the teardrops on my laptop.
What's Tim McGraw got that I don't got?

Taylor

# Yes, I Cheated on You

Is that what you wanted to hear?
Because deep down you know that
it's true, right? Clearly I'm unfaithful.

No, I didn't cheat on you, dipshit,
but I will if you keep it up. Stop
looking for the signs that aren't

there—sexts and e-mails, late night
phone calls—excuses to be unhappy.
If I wanted to fuck somebody else

I'd dump your ass. Where do you
suppose I would find the time to
cheat on you? The fourteen hours

a week we do not spend together
perhaps? Or maybe when you're
in the bathroom? Yeah, that has

to be it: I can't wait for you to
go to the bathroom so I can sneak
off and fuck my other girlfriend.

If only you had a smaller bladder,
I could cheat on you more often.

# Bull Fight

We are each both bull and matador, proud,
swinging our capes meaninglessly, fuming,
foaming at the mouth, barely dodging the
point of being gored by our sharpened horns.

*Ole!* in the ring and in the grandstands.
*Ole!* in the heat of the Spanish sun.
*Ole!* in the crisp air conditioning
of the museums, the car, our hotel.

*Ole!* from the mouth of our elderly
tour guide, Juan, afraid of being struck down
by a stray hoof or an errant sword swipe.
*Ole!* from those we call or send postcards.

*Ole!* in the plane on our flight back home;
we kill ourselves rather than die alone.

# Truth or Dare

How many guys have you slept with?

*I dare you to chug the rest of that bottle.*

Were any of them better than me?

*I dare you to go pee off your balcony.*

Who was your first?

*I dare you to do a shot of each kind of liquor you have.*

Are you still in love with your ex-boyfriend?

*I dare you to give me a hickey on my ass.*

How many guys have you really slept with?

*I dare you to run naked to the end of the block.*

Where were you last night?

*I dare you to stop being such a little bitch.*

Why are we still dating?

*I dare you to break up with me*

# You and Me and the Absurd Amount of Baggage You Brought into This Relationship Makes Three

Toothbrush: check. Deodorant: check.
Passport: check. Travel-size carton
of Q-tips: check. Mini-toothpaste: check.
Regular-size toothpaste: check. Book
to read on the plane there: check. Book to read
by the pool: check. Book to read inside

the hotel room just in case you've finished
the other books and it's raining, so swimming
and/or sunbathing are no longer options: check.
Book to read on the plane coming back: check.
Nintendo DS: check. Six Nintendo DS games,
one of which might actually be played: check.

Three bathing suits: check. A number of shirts
equal to six times the total number of days
that you're going to be gone: check. A number
of bottoms equal to at least four times the total
number of days that you're going to be
gone: check. A number of socks equal to three

times the number of days that you're going to be
gone and then multiplied by two: check.
Calculator: check. Enough underwear to survive

nuclear winter: check. Four pairs of flip flops,
all the same color: check. Five other pairs
of shoes, not including the pair that you'll

be wearing to the airport: check. Purse: check.
Other purse: check. Other purse: check.
Wallet: check. Backpack: check. Small
suitcase: check. Large suitcase: check.
Industrial-sized garment bag: check.
Tote: check. Makeup case: check. Cell

phone charger: check. Laptop: check.
Laptop charger: check. Nintendo DS
charger: check. Ipod: check. Ipod arm strap
just in case you go to the gym: check. Ipod
charger: check. Memories of the time you
went on this exact vacation with your last

boyfriend: check. Claims that you don't
think about him anymore, definitely don't
still love him, and none of this has anything
to do with us having a good time: check.
Desperate desire to act like his mistakes
don't affect me: check. Do you have everything?

Check.

# Finals

Sit down, shut up. Heads down, pencils up.
The time for studying has long since past.
You don't know what the difference is

between happiness and infrequent sex?
The effects of long-term exposure to
ridicule and constant nagging criticism?
What do you get when you multiply a

selfish young adult who refuses to grow up with
someone too much like himself? It is important
that you answer these questions correctly,
as this test is worth 100% of your final grade.

You will be judged on speed of response,
strength of argument, and sincerity, and
questions will always be multiple choice.

# Graduation

So we're probably gonna break up, right?

I think we should, although I'm terrible
at making decisions, so would you mind
just taking care of that for me?

    Maybe
if I lie here and think about it hard
enough, stare at your back long enough, through
sheer force of will I can convince you that
you don't even love me anymore, like
osmosis or something.

    Isn't that what
osmosis is?

    Except with water, right?

You would know.

    There just isn't any point.

I'm moving to Los Angeles after
graduation.

    I guess you could visit,
or move out, too, if you want, but you won't.

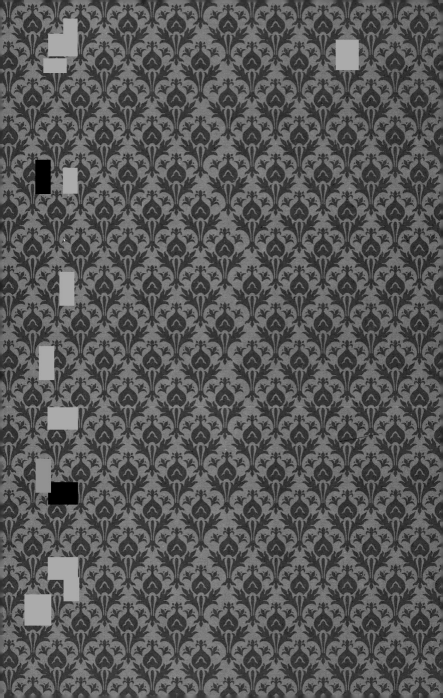

EXTREME
POVERTY
IS THE
NEW
POVERTY

# The Clown Outside
# the Furniture Store

The guy twirling a Little Caesar's Pizza
sign on the corner of Lankershim and
Vineland. Two of the five homeless dudes who

hang out under the overpass. The bus
boy at that shitty bar we'd hit up when
Mike and Andy still lived by that taco

place. Everyone in that taco place.
This gangsta-ass-looking kid I sometimes
see playing Magic when I'm picking up

my comic books, which is fucking weird on
so many levels; he has like eighteen
tattoos and he's sitting there slinging spells.

My Jiffy Lube guy. Jessica Alba.
All actors. This town is ridiculous.

# College + Love − Love = College

single guy + double(Ds + bed) + triple shots = sextuple − tuple

Dos Equis x doce botellas = veinticuatro horas hungover hombre

4 sorority girls − 3 cock blocks + \$2 wine − common sense = (9 calls/day) x 5 weeks

151 − shame + spring break − clothes = girl x girl

late night + semester abroad + (boyfriend − girlfriend)/3,000 miles = cheating x $X$, where $X$ is the number of girls who have been waiting for boyfriend to become single

tequila = girl − clothes

leaving for college + high school girlfriend = bad idea

1 weekend visiting your cousin's state school + 1 girl whose name you can't remember + 1 one-night stand = 1 case of herpes

graduation = college − money − girlfriend − excuses + responsibility + (happiness x $X$), where $X$ is the likelihood that your major will lead to a job that pays more than \$8/hour

8 x 8 x 5 = 480, before taxes

job + money + apartment + girlfriend + weekly intramural sports on a team where the oldest player went to high school with your dad = adulthood

paycheck + girlfriend = boyfriend − paycheck

beer + college = fun

beer + adulthood = weight

beer + parenthood = alcoholism

liquor + breakfast = alcoholism

6 years + 2 degrees = $120,000 in debt = alcoholism

# My Friends Who Don't Have Student Loans

Marco said let's get away fly away my dad took me once
this place man so cool I'd love to go back check it out I
met this girl there oh man so hot seriously hot body like
holy shit you would not believe let's call her up hop a
plane grab a

drink go somewhere Hong Kong Beijing Bangladesh who
cares let's go let's jet get away cool off blow some steam
can't take this man this shit this school job life shit so lame
so done I need this you need this weekend week tops
couple weeks get away Thailand Bangkok's

nice man see that girl get you one get you two shit man
fine then somewhere else anywhere Venice good no
maybe Istanbul Katmandu somewhere mountains monkeys
temples monsoons let's go let's see some shit some crazy
shit Great Wall Taj Mahal someplace

while we're still young no wife no kids no bills no rules
this is life let's go live abroad couple months year tops
anywhere anywhere do it now tell our kids grandkids
neighbor's kids write books stories man before we're
dead too old too married let's say we did

pyramids outback Singapore Shanghai Burma man
Auckland somewhere raise sheep tend bar climb shit see
shit how about eat bugs ride camels fight bulls snake boats
rickshaws jai alai just us guys this weekend maybe summer
maybe cricket maybe picture:

you me
backpacks passports
slowly learning
elephant polo.

# Part-Time Job Search

Wake up, log on, you're life's a mess:
you're on Craigslist hitting refresh.
It is boring you to death,
this part-time job search.

Though all your savings have been spent,
you know your 'rents won't help with rent.
Feeling it'll never end,
your part-time job search.

You're an adult now so don't you think it's cruel?
Forced to take jobs you had back in high school.
JCPenney by day, Chili's by night;
working overtime just to get by.

If I'm with friends and I see you
at Best Buy for an interview
I'll pretend you're shopping, too,
it's not a part-time job search.

You'd live a life of luxury
without those debts you owe Sallie;
hundred grand for a degree,
learned to part-time job search.

You'd do undercover security at the mall,
or work a country club polishing golf balls.
You would take some data entry if you could,
but they won't hire you; your resume's too good.

I've got something that I must tell,
you're not alone in low-wage hell.
I've been doing it as well,
a part-time job search.

I get excited when I see
job openings at Dairy Queen;
at least I'll get some free ice cream
from this part-time job search.
Sad to be on a part-time job search.
You and me: part-time job search.

# Hunger

Like, bloated Somali children hunger.
It's 3:18 in the morning and I
just smoked my fifth bowl of the night hunger.
The Third Horseman of the Apocalypse,
his fat ass riding a skinny little
black horse hunger. Gandhi twenty-one days
into one of his strikes hunger; and if
you only gave me crusts or orange juice
right now I'd slap you hunger. Bad enough
to put me on the list for Meals on Wheels
hunger. Whale hunger. Galactus hunger.
Waiting on line at the Wendy's drive-thru
for twenty-five fucking minutes hunger.
Okay, that one is happening right now.

# For Mama Celeste

## As a Child

Mother cut tiny
slices for my small boy hands:
delicate pizza.

## In College

Hold up. This whole time
you were only a dollar?
You cheap, frozen whore.

## After College

Sorry about that.
Please take me back, Mama C.
I'm sick of ramen.

# On the Origin of Reese's

*by Means of Natural Selection;*
*or the Preservation of Favored Tastes*
*in the Struggle for Life*

1—Variation under Domestication

Peanut butter cups
are eaten in many different ways,
depending on the home in which the cup
is found.

2—Variation under Nature

A peanut butter cup eaten
outdoors becomes soggy in the rain,
but melts if left for too long in the sun.

3—Struggle for Existence

The first cups were made by H. B. Reese back
in 1928, but he merged with
the Hershey Company in '63.

4—Natural Selection

You might enjoy Big Cups, but your sister
might prefer Dark Chocolate, or even
NutRageous bars.

5—Laws of Variation

People do not enjoy
their preferred peanut butter cups by chance,
but due to some predisposed condition.

6—Difficulties on Theory

But then, should there not be an infinite
number of peanut butter cup types and
varieties?

7—Instinct

That's my gut reaction.

8—Hybridism

There are indeed many varieties:
White Chocolate, Caramel, Inside Out,
the cute little mini-cups.

9—On the Imperfection of the Geological Record

It's quite hard
to keep track of every single cup
you've ever eaten.

10—On the Geological Succession of Organic Beings

You may not know this,
but there are actually other types
of candy in the world, and some even
contain peanut butter and chocolate.

11—On Geographical Distribution

I hear those Cadbury guys make a mean
fruit and nut bar.

12—On Geographical Distribution *continued*

It is interesting
to note, however, that Hershey's holds a
license to manufacture Cadbury
chocolate products in the USA.

13—Mutual Affinities of Organic Beings: Morphology:
Embryology: Rudimentary Organs

Good chocolate is just good chocolate.

14—Recapitulation and Conclusion

Almost all confections today retain
a common sugary ancestor, and
many still claim direct descent from milk,
cocoa beans, and George Washington Carver.

# Why Do Buses Smell?

The young girl asks her
mother. I listen, because
I want to know, too.

# Ode to Arizona, I Guess

The beverage company. Not because
I don't like the state. It's a dry heat, yeah,
we get it. And also not because I
dislike Snapple. The majority of
this poem is about Snapple, the sweet
sucrose tea of my youth. Arizona,
I love you because you are cheap and I
am poor. You're the golden-hearted hooker
of the beverage world. 99¢
for those giant cans at convenience stores;
99¢ for liter-plus bottles
at respectable discount grocery
barns; massive jugs of slightly racist green
tea for the cost of one Diet Snapple.
But isn't it worth it to splurge for the
best stuff on Earth? Choices! Lemon Tea! Green
Tea! Pineapple Peach Mango Oolong Tea,
whatever the fuck that is! I don't care,
it's an option when I can afford it.
There used to be this flavor, Snapricot
Orange, looked like piss, tasted like gold would
taste if God distilled it as a juice drink
that rained down from Heaven. Paired with shitty
amazing boardwalk pizza it was worth
the $2.50. I had money to spare!
Okay, my parents had money to spare!
Cases of the good stuff, bottles never
recycled. Not now, I've crossed the border.

# My Second Dream Involving Bruce Willis

This Week. I'm his sidekick in the fifth
*Die Hard* movie, but it's secretly a remake
of *Die Hard 2: Die Harder.*

Snow, airport, military, random guys
on snowmobiles shooting everyone.
Great time for all involved. Except,
when I get captured by extras-as-terrorists,
instead of coming up with an elaborate
plan to rescue me from the burnt out
schoolhouse taking the thematic place
of *DH2:DHer*'s church explosion,
old Bruno hops in a 'vette and decides
to just run the bad guys over. And then
back up. And then run them over again.
And he's smoking a cigar. And laughing.
And some hot chick who is decidedly NOT
his wife Holly is half-naked in the back seat.
And he's yelling at me through the window,
things like, *Get in the car, kid, before I shoot
you in the ass!* and *Ramona Flowers
isn't my real daughter, she's a comic
book character, ya perv!* but with love.

# Modern-Day Heroics

I killed a spider today, which made me sad
because I absolutely hate killing spiders.
I like to think they'll protect me if
the ghosts of all the bugs I've killed
ever come back to haunt me. Plus,
Spider-man is a spider, so . . .

Anyway, it was actually a girl's fault,
as most things tend to be. Me, girl, bed, etc.,
spider, wall, scream, etc., calm, logic, batshit
crazy, etc., shoe, death, hero, sex reward.
I don't recommend annihilating vermin as a
consistent form of increasing the heart rate of
whoever is in your bed— I'm not proud of what
I've done—but Goddamn, was it effective.

# (American) Ninja Warrior

I bet I could kick your ass.
*(Not me, the protagonist of this poem.*
He *bets he could kick your ass.*
*I can hardly kick dirt off my shoe.)*
I'll kick your ass so hard you'll
be shitting through your nose.
*(Again, not me. That sounds*
*pretty fucking gross, actually.)*
I'll kick your ass, and then,
when the cops come, I'll run
away, but not like some little
sissy-ass street thug runs away.
I'll run away like the fucking
ninja warrior that I am *(he isn't)*
and do back flips off of cars
and climb up walls and taunt
the fucking pigs from the rooftops
as I do fifty—nay, one hundred
one-handed push-ups while
giving them the middle finger.
They won't be able to catch me
because I'm a ninja warrior,
and I can do crazy French power-
walking shit that normal people
are too stupid and normal to do.
*(Seriously, though, I couldn't*
*do half the stuff those parkour*
*guys do. Sometimes I can fly*

*in my dreams. That's about*
*as close as I can get, really.)*
And you know what else?
FUCK YOU, AMERICAN
GLADIATORS! My show
kicks your show's ass! Yeah!
*(Okay, now he's gone too far.)*

# Cleaning Off My George Foreman Grill

But thinking about moving back home,
where I know real people, with real grills
in their backyards, behind the houses that
they own. And thinking also about the meals
that I cook for myself—grilled cheese;
Chunky Chicken Noodle; Banquet dinners;
burgers, maybe; pork chops with mashed
potatoes every once in a while, if I'm
feeling ambitious—and about how easy
it would be to let my mother start cooking
for me again. Meat loaf; tacos; grilled steak;
fried chicken with corn and buttered noodles.
My family expects me to announce it any day,
that I'm coming home again, for good. Not yet.

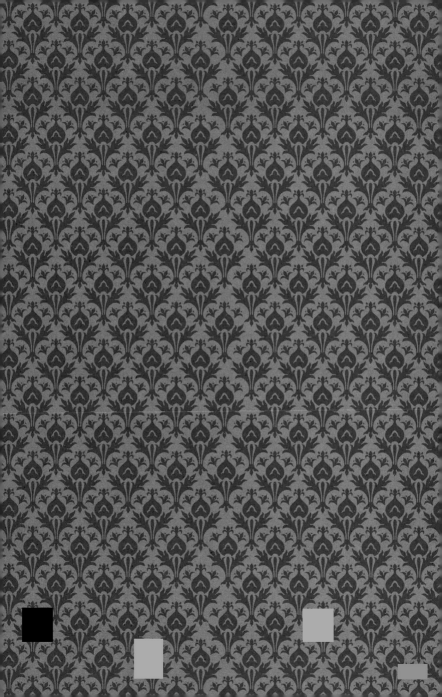

# TWENTY-FIVE
# TO LIFE

# Former Future Lover

I'd love to say you're ugly now. You're not.

Our made-up future children
would be proud. It's funny
to be saying this aloud: I used to super
crush on you a lot. For serious,
back in the day I vowed to maybe somehow
admit that I felt goofy even looking at you:
You'd melt beneath my soulful gaze;
confess a cloud had been lifted

from your brow, your heart dealt
a healthy, romantic blow, my words
bringing you a pink blow-up raft you could
cling to in life's gross public pool,
a seat belt in love's Jeep. Anyway,
it was nothing. Congratulations,
it's a lovely ring.

# Bigfoot Is Real
# (and Other Absurdities)

Han shot first.
UFOs landed at Roswell.
The Loch Ness Monster is a horse.
I can eat 6 saltines in under a minute.
Bloody Mary, Bloody Mary, Bloody Mary.
There are alligators in the sewers of New York.
Diet Dr. Pepper tastes just like regular Dr. Pepper.

Gonzo is a Fraggle.
Hulk can beat up Blackbolt.
The door is open, but the ride ain't free.
Chivalry is dead.
Paul is dead.

God is dead.
You never loved me.

# Do You Believe in Magic?

Now, I won't name names,
but some people get sucked into trading card games,
ones like Magic. Or have you ever maybe
spent three straight days on your MMORPG?
I'd lend you a bunch of Magic cards and dice to roll,
but it's like teaching necromancy to a mountain troll.

If you believe in Magic, slaying demons and orcs,
chilling in Mom's basement with a bunch of dorks,
reading Tolkien, rewatching *Dr. Who*,
I can't really condemn you because I've been there, too.
Your geek bar's risen past an Asimov moon,
kill streak longer than summer on Dune.

If you believe in Magic, come along with me;
we'll raid until morning if you're too tired to sleep.
And maybe, if we time it just right,
the kids in Japan will sign on for the night
and we'll keep playing, baby, 'til we're banned
from the forums of that online *Settlers of Catan*.

Yeah, do you believe in Magic?
Believe in the Magic of co-op *Halo*.
Believe in the Magic of lucky rolls.
Believe in the Magic when your rent's still free.
Oh, talking 'bout Magic:

The Gathering.

101

# Ode to My Girlfriend's Boyfriend

Someday I'd like to be the other man,
the celebrity exception to a monogamous
relationship. The one whose address is
googled extensively so that a gaggle of girls
can happen to be jogging past my front door
as I leave to buy Golden Grahams or porn.

In short, I would like to be you, Jesse McCartney,
a million voices calling for me,
body like music to my girlfriend's ears.
She spent months singing "Leavin'" to me
in her car, to the point where I began
to think she was practicing for the day
when she'd be never coming back again frealz
because you finally found her beautiful soul.

Seriously though, all that I hear from her friends
again and again are compliments about you.
*OMG at his concert we saw this lady*
*and her daughter both had JMAC tattoos!*
How do you stay away knowing all these girls
are so into you? Tell me that you're getting
no sleep or at least have a biddy every
night with you, because I know you've got
one lying right here next to me.

# My Brother at Fourteen

Has already had more girlfriends than
I'm most likely ever going to;
has already sprayed more Axe body
spray than I'm definitely ever
going to; has already pissed off
more future gang members and young drug

dealers than I expect
is wise for a boy his
age, though I commend him
on his dedication
to being an equal
opportunity douche.
I know he'll succeed in
whatever he does, though.
He's a smart, driven kid.
That, and I'll kick his ass
if he fucks up too bad.

# Escape Route

What're you more afraid of, zombie plagues
or tidal waves? Aliens or earthquakes?
Lava flash floods? Spontaneous combustion?
Werewolf terrorists? Tornadoes from the Black
Lagoon? What's your contingency plan?

You should have a bag prepared, filled
with emergency supplies: water, flashlights,
batteries, matches, NASA food pouches,
one of those funky space blankets maybe,
a whistle, some rope, a deck of cards.

Or better yet, scratch these words from
your list of acceptable adjectives describing
a potential home: rural, isolated, hot, cold,
populous, Southwestern, Transylvanian.
Unless you don't have a problem dying unexpectedly.

You should probably avoid cities altogether,
too many unnecessary dangers. Rioting, disease,
economic collapse, subway accidents, indigenous
populations of subterranean mole people,
rat infestation, terrorism, Scientology.

I guess you can't live by the coast, though, either:
tidal waves, tsunamis, asteroid impacts causing
sheer walls of salty water eighty stories tall
to descend upon your home, mutant jellyfish.
But honestly, who'd want to live away from the ocean?

Can't go to Japan (Godzilla), China (communists),
Russia (Russians), or anywhere that's too hot
for fear of constant ultraviolet exposure.
Definitely don't go to California, ever. Deathtrap.
Australia's nice, if you want dingoes to eat your baby.

There's no escaping it; you are going to die
where you live unless you find a way to escape
to somewhere less deadly, though it's fairly
safe to assume you've got a good chance of
dying there, too. Not gonna lie, it sucks to be you.

# And You'll Be Way Cooler in College

Listen, kid, I know life sucks.
I know you'd rather be anywhere
but where you are, no matter
where you go. I know nobody
listens, nobody cares, nobody's
got it as bad as you. It's true.
Everyone else is full of shit, because
their problems can't possibly be
half as bad as yours, and if they
say they are, they're making it up.
I know, trust me, they all suck.
It hurts, and it hurts that it hurts,
and it hurts that you have to admit
that it hurts because hurting is weak
and hurting is stupid and hurting
is pointless because there's so much
stuff you could be doing right now
if only it didn't hurt so much
all the time and maybe if you
were a little better looking and
if someone would only just give
you the chance and some money
you could do something with yourself
because it's not that you don't
want to or don't care because
you do care, you care too much.

And you would be fucking great,
the best the world has ever seen,
if only someone would give you
half a chance. I know. Life sucks.
There's not much you can do.

# Obligatory Party Commentary

*OMG, Rachel, you still have MySpace?!*
*I totally didn't even know what that was*
*when you said it, I forgot it ever existed!*
*No, I mean it's cool. They did some study,*
*though, and, like, only poor people use it.*
*Less poor people use Facebook, although*
*I'm already so over Facebook. Twitter*
*is so much more professional. And I was*
*reading this tweet the other day actually*
*about blah blah blah Obama? I could not*
*believe it. Blah blah blah gay healthcare!*
*And Rico was telling me this blog he*
*blahblahblech and yeah the border.*
*So crazy. I heard blahdiladifuckingda,*
*too, but only in West Virginia. Blahoils*
*blechmilfBPblearghonadiethnxnothe Pentagon*
*blahblahso overrated. How's your new job?*
*I've been working with—OMG, Bethany!*

# He's in Miami

Just in case the Los Angeles Police Department
is looking for information on the whereabouts of
a crafty-looking Latino male, age 30, about 5'10"
and extremely skinny, who likes to smoke pot
(a lot) and play video games all day, and who
enjoys drinking Newcastle, Guinness, and high
quantities of Vitamin Water, in the interests of
any ongoing drug-related crimes in the area, for
example, illegal possession, illegal sale, or illegal
production in his friend's apartment in Los Feliz,
he's in Miami.

If you manage to track him down, please let me
know. He owes me rent, two bottles of Arizona
Green Tea, and a frozen pizza. Supreme, please.

# Sans Roommate

Sans patience, sans money, sans
the emotional capacity to scour
the dregs of Craigslist one last time,

not to find someone who's perfect,
not someone who's going to be
my best friend, my best man, my

heterosexual life partner during
my time in Los Angeles before I
ultimately move back home anyway,

for God's sake just someone even
remotely normal, not a complete
fucking creeper. Do you have a

history of addiction? Mental disease?
Kleptomania? A foot fetish? Do
you like to stand over strangers

while they're sleeping at night?
Are you secretly growing pot in
a newly remodeled loft across town?

Will you respond to my ad within
minutes and then fail to write back
when I try to make plans to show

you the apartment? Do you not bathe?
Are you forty-seven years old with
two toddlers and a dog? Would you

describe yourself as *bipolar,*
*agoraphobic,* or *unemployed*?
Do you have cats, plural?

THEN I DO NOT WANT TO LIVE
WITH YOU SO STOP E-MAILING ME
PLEASE FOR THE LOVE OF GOD!

# Your Friend Who Dates the Younger Girls

She moves lithely, smooth, and opens her mouth
wide when she speaks, unless she's chewing gum,
but still then the slight angle of her jaw
and wetness of her lips makes her even
more appealing to the thirteen-year-old

inside. She's never tired, and I'm sure could
go all night if her parents weren't so strict.
Age is just a number, like twenty-five
to life, or seventeen candles, or four
more years until she can hang out in bars.

I remember *Rugrats* back before they
got growed up, on Snick Saturdays with *Doug*,
and *Are You Afraid of the Dark?*—she is—
wanting my own big orange couch; and I
remember thinking Winona Ryder

was so old in *Great Balls of Fire*, not
understanding what the big deal was;
and I remember the 80s: Does she?
Don't answer that. There's nothing wrong with a
little range. What will it matter in ten

years, after marriage? You'll be better off,
beating life on both ends of the spectrum:
still getting those girls you weren't finished with
in high school; dying twelve years before your
wife; thinking no one will ever leave you.

# Impact

I am making eggs, and waking up much
earlier than I would normally choose, and
also leaving the apartment in the morning,
before the slits of light shining through
the blinds would have naturally blinded me
awake anyway, and now that I mention it,
I am leaving the apartment *at all*, which I
am loath to do these days, since I am
jobless, prospectless, hopelessly skirting
around inevitable acceptance of the fact
        —brace yourself—
that I might have to take a position less
than perfect for my particular skill set,
i.e., I am flat fucking broke, folks, and can
no longer afford to leave the peace and
relatively inexpensive quiet of my slowly
mold-growing cave of a home, but I go,

and not only do I go, I go to drink beer, lots
of beer, and I go to eat chicken fingers, and
most likely mozzarella sticks, and maybe wings
if someone else orders wings; I go to spend
money, because it is Sunday, it is fall, it is football.

# Why You Should Listen
# to Classical Music

Two words: John Fucking Williams.
*Jaws. Superman. Indiana Jones.*
When Darth Maul gets chopped
in half (::spoiler alert::), Obi Wan
is grooving to some classical music.

I know what you're thinking, though:
*Listen, jackass, that movie came out*
*in 1999. That's not classical music.*
First: Do you know what a leitmotif is?
Second: Little Johnny Love is like
eighty years old. Classical music.

Fine, better example: Richard Wagner.
Yeah, you know what, maybe he
hated the Jews a bit, had a little
Mel Gibson kinda thing going on.
I'm not gonna lie, I still enjoy watching
*Lethal Weapon 2.* I won't go buy it on
Blu-ray anytime soon, but if it's on TBS,
my ass is in the chair. Wagner's like that.
Ghosts, trolls, frost giants, godsex,
Vikings, demons, classical music.

But back to John Williams for a second:
The guy's got range. Did you know he
composed the music for four separate
Olympic Games and the theme song
to *Lost in Space*?! He's ridiculous.

So what if it puts you to sleep?
Listen when you're going to bed, then!
Start with Tchaikovsky's first
piano concerto (though not if you're
going to bed), or just watch *Fantasia*;
Mahler and Debussy are pretty gangster;
anything by Mozart, obviously.
I'm assuming you haven't seen *Amadeus*,
or else we wouldn't even need to have
this conversation, would we?

Classical music. It makes you smarter.
And admit it, you could be more cultured;
you just picked up a book called *Broetry*.

# Your Name Here

*That was so much fun! We should start hanging*
*out with your friends more often. But who was*
*that _____ girl I saw you talking*
*to before? Do you know her? How did you*
*guys meet? Seriously, you did not just*
*meet her. She was acting like she's known you*
*forever, like you're best friends or something.*
*Come on, she was all over you. Okay,*
*if you say so, but I know what I saw.*

—

*Ugh, we should not have opened that second*
*bottle of wine, I'm a little tipsy.*
*It was good to get everybody*
*together, though. I bet you were glad that*
*that _____ girl was there? Don't even*
*try it, her eyes lit up like Christmas the*
*moment you walked through the door. Did you know*
*she was coming out with us? So you have*
*not talked to her once since that night? Yeah, sure.*

—

*I am so beat, we should go right to bed*
*when we get home. Huh? No, I'm fine. I just*
*want to go to sleep. Those guys can be so*
*exhausting sometimes, I don't know how you*

*can deal with them. And that _____ girl;*
*she's so annoying! Does she ever stop*
*talking for more than like fifteen seconds?*
*Everyone thinks she's the greatest thing.*
*She's not even that cute. Stupid slutbag.*

—

*Thank God, I thought we would never get out*
*of there. Wait, what? Hold on, you call that fun?*
*Sitting with a bunch of drunks all night and*
*hearing the same stupid stories they tell*
*every fucking time we see them. Fun.*
*Well, of course. That _____ girl, little*
*miss perfect, she was on your arm all night,*
*wasn't she? No, fuck you, don't act like you*
*don't like the attention. You're an asshole.*

—

*I told you already, I'm not going*
*anywhere tonight. Because I don't feel*
*like it. Excuse me? No, I don't feel like*
*being embarrassed while some bimbo crawls*
*all over you. I'm not in the mood, thanks.*
*That _____ girl, you dumb shit! Deny*
*it all you want, but I know that something's*
*going on between you two, I can tell.*
*'Cus I'm not a fucking moron, dickhead.*

—

*No, no, we broke up. I don't know, he was*
*a lying asshat, how's that? He didn't*
*even have the decency to admit*
*that he was cheating on me, even once*
*he knew we were done. Like, grow some fucking*
*balls, dirtbag! Whatever, I'm better off.*
*I'm just pissed it was that _____ girl.*
*Fuck her. But it's not like I was going*
*to marry the bastard anyway, right?*

# Quarter-Life Crisis

Unless I somehow live beyond the
expected 78.4
years—74.6, really,
I was born in 1985,
and even less because I'm a male….
Okay, so unless I somehow live
*well* beyond predictions, this is more
like a third-life crisis, though without
the two extra lives that I should get.

So I'm
behind.

I guess that means I have a lot
of catching up to do. I should
be: confronting mortality
more; reminiscing about stuff;
realizing that my friends are
not as talented as I thought;
more lonely, more depressed, maybe
more suicidal or something.

Since I started late,
though, I think I might
kick ass instead. Plus,
that all sounds kinda
boring anyway.

# Index

**125**

# Thank God . . .

. . . for Jason Rekulak and everyone else at Quirk Books.

. . . for the spectacular illustrations of Lars Leetaru.

. . . for Amy Gerstler, a master poetess, for her inspiration and advice.

. . . for everyone who read early broetic drafts, but especially Suzanne Parker, Brad Rochefort, Josh Jacobson, April Dávila, Emily Zilm, and Thom Fucking Dunn.

. . . for Emma Watson. Always.

... for USC's Master of Professional Writing program, where broetry was born, and for Brighde Mullins, Dinah Lenney, Chris Meeks, and Nan Cohen, who helped to raise the little bastard.

... for Marvel Comics, without which I might possibly lose interest in planet Earth.

... for Jeff Stokely, Melanie Yarbrough, and Rupa dasGupta, who provided me with important broetical assistance at various times throughout my writing.

... for my parents, grandparents, aunts, and uncles, who drilled it into my head that I could grow up to be anything I wanted, even though I assume they meant astronaut or president, not poet.

... for my brothers and sisters, whose relative boredom or lack thereof was the standard by which I judged the quality of many of these pages.

... for the fine folks at Archaia Comics, who helped me determine that I absolutely, 100% wanted to be a writer and nothing else.

... for good poetry, which inspires me to write.

... for bad poetry, which inspires me to write way more than good poetry does.

... for God.

... for Guinness.

... for *Armageddon*.